Debates on 20th-Century Immigration

Melissa Abramovitz

ReferencePoint Press®

San Diego, CA

About the Author

Melissa Abramovitz is an award-winning author/freelance writer who specializes in writing educational nonfiction books and magazine articles for all age groups, from preschoolers through adults. She has published hundreds of magazine articles and more than fifty educational books for children and teenagers, and also writes short stories, poems, picture books, and books for authors. Abramovitz graduated summa cum laude from the University of California, San Diego, with a degree in psychology and is also a graduate of the Institute of Children's Literature.

For more information, contact:
ReferencePoint Press, Inc.
PO Box 27779
San Diego, CA 92198
www.ReferencePointPress.com

Picture Credits:

Cover: Everett Historical/Shutterstock.com

6: Zack Frank/Shutterstock.com (bottom left)
6: Everett Historical/Shutterstock.com (top right)
7: Everett Historical/Shutterstock.com (bottom left)
7: Victor Mascheck/Shutterstock.com (bottom right)
7: VallarieE/iStock.com (top right)
11: Maury Aaseng

19: Edward Lara/Shutterstock.com
26: David Litman/Shutterstock.com
32: Miami Police Department mug shot of Al Capone, 1930 (b/w photo)/HistoryMiami, Florida, USA/Bridgeman Images
38: Juan Carlos Tinjaca/Shutterstock.com
46: Everett Historical/Shutterstock.com
55: Kamira/Shutterstock.com
60: Diego Cervo/Shutterstock.com
67: Blend Images/Shutterstock.com

LIBRARY OF CONGRESS CATALOGING-IN-PUBLICATION DATA

Name: Melissa Abramovitz, author.
Title: Debates on 20th-Century Immigration/by Melissa Abramovitz.
Description: San Diego, CA: ReferencePoint Press, Inc., 2019. | Series: Debating History | Includes bibliographical references and index.
Identifiers: ISBN 9781682823705 (eBook) | ISBN 9781682823699 (hardback)
Subjects: LCSH: Immigration—Juvenile literature. |
 Immigration—United States—History—20th century—Juvenile literature.

Contents

Is slavery immoral?

No thinking person today would argue that slavery is moral. Yet in the United States in the early and mid-1800s, slavery was an accepted institution in the southern states. While many southerners never owned slaves, the institution of slavery had widespread support from plantation owners, elected officials, and even the general populace. Its defenders were often respected members of their communities. For instance, John C. Calhoun—a US senator from South Carolina—was a staunch defender of slavery. He believed that enslaved Africans benefited from their status as slaves—and said as much during an 1837 Senate speech. "Never before," he stated, "has the black race of Central Africa, from the dawn of history to the present day, attained a condition so civilized and so improved, not only physically, but morally and intellectually."

Statements like this might be confounding and hurtful today. But a true understanding of history—especially of those events that have altered daily life and human communities—requires students to become familiar with the thoughts, attitudes, and beliefs of the people who lived these events. Only by examining various perspectives will students truly understand the past and be able to make sound judgments about the future.

This is the goal of the *Debating History* series. Through a narrative-driven, pro/con format, the series introduces students to some of the complex issues that have dominated public discourse over the decades—topics such as the slave trade, twentieth-century immigration, the Soviet Union's collapse, and the rise of Islamist extremism. All chapters revolve around a single, pointed question, such as the following:

- Is slavery immoral?
- Do immigrants threaten American culture and values?
- Did the arms race cause the Soviet Union's collapse?
- Does poverty cause Islamist extremism?

This inquiry-based approach to history introduces student researchers to core issues and concerns on a given topic. Each chapter includes one part that argues the affirmative and one part that argues the negative—all written by a single author. With the single-author format, the predominant arguments for and against an issue can be synthesized into clear, accessible discussions supported by details and evidence, including relevant facts, quotes, and examples. All volumes include focus questions to guide students as they read each pro/con discussion, a visual chronology, and a list of sources for conducting further research.

This approach reflects the guiding principles set out in the College, Career, and Civic Life (C3) Framework for Social Studies State Standards developed by the National Council for the Social Studies. "History is interpretive," the framework's authors write. "Even if they are eyewitnesses, people construct different accounts of the same event, which are shaped by their perspectives—their ideas, attitudes, and beliefs. Historical understanding requires recognizing this multiplicity of points of view in the past. . . . It also requires recognizing that perspectives change over time, so that historical understanding requires developing a sense of empathy with people in the past whose perspectives might be very different from those of today." The *Debating History* series supports these goals by providing a solid introduction to the study of pro/con issues in history.

Important Events of 20th-Century Immigration

1875
Congress passes the Page Act, which prohibits people deemed to be morally corrupt from immigrating to the United States.

1929
The start of the Great Depression results in drastic declines in the number of immigrants to the United States because no jobs are available.

1902
Congress extends the 1882 Chinese Exclusion Act, which bans immigrants from China.

1921
The Immigration Act of 1921 imposes immigration quotas based on national origin; it favors people from Western Europe.

1885   1895   1905   1915   1925   1935

1903
The poem "The New Colossus" is inscribed on a bronze plaque inside the Statue of Liberty's pedestal; it becomes a symbol of America's role as a haven for the oppressed and disadvantaged.

1933
The US government establishes the Immigration and Naturalization Service to regulate and control immigration on a national level.

1917
The Immigration Act of 1917 takes effect; it requires potential immigrants to pass a literacy test and prohibits immigration by anyone from certain Asian and Middle Eastern countries.

1924
The Immigration Act of 1924 reduces the quotas based on national origin for immigrants from Eastern and Southern Europe. Congress also establishes the US Border Patrol to prevent illegal immigration.

1986
The Immigration Control and Reform Act imposes penalties on employers who hire illegal immigrants, offers amnesty to those who meet certain requirements, and authorizes increased Border Patrol funding.

1952
The Immigration and Naturalization Act encourages immigrants with high levels of education and skills that could benefit America to come to the United States.

1950
The Internal Security Act bans immigrants affiliated with the Communist or Fascist Parties.

1995
Congress allocates (through a lottery system) fifty-five thousand immigration visas for a new category of immigrants called diversity immigrants.

1965
The Immigration Act of 1965 eliminates national origin quotas and makes reunifying immigrant families a priority.

| 1945 | 1955 | 1965 | 1975 | 1985 | 1995 | 2005 |

1945
World War II ends, resulting in hundreds of thousands of Nazi concentration camp survivors and refugees from Nazi-occupied countries asking for immigration visas.

1976
The Immigration Act of 1976 places restrictions on the number of immigrants from Western Hemisphere countries, leading to increases in illegal immigration.

1990
The Immigration Reform and Control Act of 1990 raises the number of skilled workers and lowers the number of unskilled workers allowed to immigrate.

1980
More than 120,000 Cuban immigrants, including many criminals released from prisons, arrive in the United States via the Mariel boatlift.

Chapter One

A Brief History of 20th-Century Immigration

Immigration has been a controversial topic in the United States for a long time. Concerns about immigration follow a basic pattern: One generation of immigrants usually questions whether the next generation to arrive will benefit or hurt the US economy and way of life, whether they are doing enough to assimilate, and whether the government should limit their numbers. This pattern has occurred over many years, but immigration concerns intensified during the 20th century, which saw several large waves of immigration to the United States. As sociology professor David Heer wrote in 1996, "One of the most contentious issues facing the United States today is immigration policy."[1]

Early Immigration Policies

Immigration policies during early American history were uncomplicated and limited. The Constitution that was ratified in 1790 allowed "any alien, being a free white person of good character" who lived in the United States for two years to become a citizen after taking an oath in court "to support the constitution of the United States."[2] These new citizens were also required to renounce any foreign allegiance. In 1895 the criteria for naturalization (the process through which a foreign-born person becomes a citizen) were changed to require five years of lawful residence in the United States. The first limits on the number and ethnicity of immigrants were also imposed in the late 1800s and early 1900s as concerns grew about the effects of rising numbers of immigrants on American society.

Immigration Waves

Historians and social scientists divide periods of mass immigration to the United States into waves. The first wave occurred between the 1700s and 1820 and included mainly Caucasian, English-speaking Protestant immigrants from Great Britain and Western and Northern Europe. The second wave occurred in the 1840s and 1850s and included mostly Germans and Irish Catholics. The third wave, between 1880 and 1914, brought many non-English-speaking Catholics and Jews from Eastern and Southern Europe. The fourth wave, which began in the mid-1960s, included mostly immigrants and refugees from Mexico, Central America, Asia, and Africa.

> "One of the most contentious issues facing the United States today is immigration policy."[1]
>
> —Sociology professor David Heer

Immigrants who arrived during the first wave mostly sought religious freedom and economic opportunity. Those who arrived during the second and third waves were often driven by desperation to escape starvation or religious persecution or by a desire to get rich. The potato famine in Ireland in the mid-1840s, for example, led more than one and a half million Irish, mostly Catholics, to immigrate to the United States between 1841 and 1860. Pogroms (targeted violence) against Jews in Russia and other areas of Eastern Europe brought hundreds of thousands of Jews to America between 1875 and 1920. The California Gold Rush, which started in 1848, and the need for workers to build the transcontinental railroad also brought thousands of Chinese immigrants during the mid-1800s.

Immigration Restriction

Prejudice against non-Anglo, non-Protestant newcomers contributed to restrictive immigration policies. In 1849, for instance, Americans who resented Irish Catholic immigrants formed a secret organization called the Order of the Star Spangled Banner, which later became known as the Know-Nothing Party. This group voted for lawmakers who supported restricting immigration of non-Protestants and nonwhites. Other groups that resented Chinese immigrants pressured Congress to pass the Chinese Exclusion Act in 1882. This law banned Chinese people from entering the United States or becoming citizens for the next ten years. It was extended in 1892 and then made permanent in 1902.

Congress enacted the Chinese Exclusion Act in response to widespread fears, particularly in western states, about the large numbers of Chinese workers who arrived during the Gold Rush and railroad-building era. Many native-born Americans believed these workers were contributing to unemployment and decreasing wages because they were willing to work for low wages. Many also thought the Chinese were racially and morally inferior to Caucasians and would genetically and culturally corrupt American society if allowed to immigrate en masse. During congressional debates in 1870, for example, Senator George Williams of Oregon urged his fellow senators to restrict Chinese immigration because "whenever the Mongolians or Chinese become numerous and powerful in this country, we may look for tumult . . . conflict . . . ignorance, idolatry, immorality, vice, [and] disease."[3] Besides leading to passage of the Chinese Exclusion Acts, these sentiments foreshadowed later ethnic restrictions on immigration.

Further Immigration Restrictions

In the early 20th century, groups like the Immigration Restriction League advocated using literacy tests to further restrict immigration by non-English-speakers. After three US presidents vetoed proposed literacy requirements, literacy tests were finally implemented in 1917. Around this time, books that expressed alarm

A Snapshot of 20th-Century US Immigration

In the century between 1900 and 2000, the number of immigrants living in the United States nearly tripled, from 10.3 million in 1900 to 28.4 million in 2000. The biggest jump in immigration took place between 1970 and 2000, a result of changes in immigration laws in the mid-1960s and other factors. In their 2001 report, researchers from the Center for Immigration Studies noted that this increase was higher than at any other time in history.

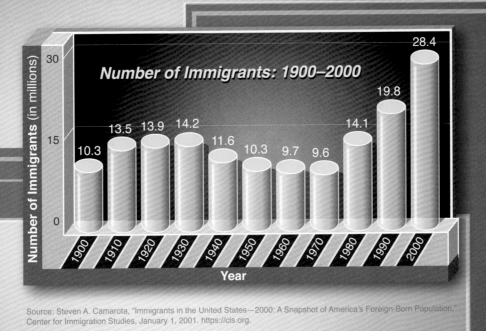

Number of Immigrants: 1900–2000

Source: Steven A. Camarota, "Immigrants in the United States—2000: A Snapshot of America's Foreign-Born Population," Center for Immigration Studies, January 1, 2001. https://cis.org.

about nonwhite, non-Protestant immigrants corrupting American culture and weakening the Caucasian gene pool fanned popular fears and led to demands for even tighter immigration restrictions.

In response to such fears Congress implemented ethnic immigration restrictions in 1924. The 1924 law completely banned immigration from Asia and created national-origin quotas. Under these quotas, 2 percent of the total number of people of each nationality already in the United States as of the 1890 national census would be allowed to enter the country as immigrants. These quotas favored immigrants from Northern and Western Europe (the United Kingdom, Germany, and Ireland, in particular) because most immigrants to that point had come from these areas. As the US State Department's Office of the Historian explains, "In all of its parts, the most basic purpose of the 1924 Immigration Act was to preserve the ideal of U.S. homogeneity."[4]

By the time World War II began in 1939, immigration to the United States had slowed considerably, in part because of job losses during the Great Depression. Even so, anti-immigrant sentiment was widespread. Immigrant advocates urged the US government to waive existing quotas and accept more refugees from Nazi concentration camps and war-torn Europe, but this did not happen. One survey conducted in 1939 found that 83 percent of Americans opposed accepting additional refugee immigrants, and the government did not defy this widespread opposition. President Franklin Roosevelt refused to let ships carrying these refugees land in America, and many people were sent back to Europe to perish.

The Fourth Wave

The next massive immigration wave began as a result of the Immigration and Nationality Act of 1965. That law removed national-origin quotas on the grounds that they were discriminatory, instead focusing on reunifying immigrant families. Immigrants were allowed to bring in relatives, who could then bring in other relatives. Lawmakers like Senator Edward Kennedy of Massachusetts asserted that family reunification policies would not change existing immigration levels, but in reality these policies led to unprecedented numbers of new immigrants from around the world, particularly from Latin America, Asia, Africa, and the Caribbean. In 1960 more than 50 percent of the immigrants to the United States came from Europe, 6 percent came from Asia, and 9 percent from Latin America. Between 1981 and 1990, 10 percent came from Europe, 37 percent came from Asia, and 42 percent came from Latin America.

The 1965 law also allowed anyone who feared persecution if they returned to their home country to stay in the United States either temporarily or permanently, depending on the country of origin. For instance, hundreds of thousands of immigrants from Indo-Chinese Communist countries were allowed to stay in the United States permanently after the Vietnam War ended in 1975.

Overall 3.5 million legal immigrants entered the United States between 1963 and 1972, and 9 million arrived between 1982 and 1992. The overwhelming majority settled in California, New York, Florida, Texas, Illinois, and New Jersey. By 1985 more than 25 percent of the populations of Los Angeles, New York City, and Miami were foreign-born.

Overwhelmed by Immigrants

The number of illegal immigrants also grew. The Immigration and Naturalization Service (INS) estimated there were 6 million to 12 million undocumented immigrants in the United States by 1974. Several government agencies have estimated that the number of illegal immigrants grew by approximately 8 percent each year between 1970 and 2000. Congress passed the Immigration Reform and Control Act of 1986 in an attempt to reduce this growing problem by imposing sanctions on employers who hired illegal immigrants. Once employers stopped hiring them, lawmakers reasoned, illegal immigration would stop. At the same time the act offered amnesty (permanent legal resident status) to 2.71 million illegal immigrants and status as legal agricultural workers to an additional 1.1 million.

Still, these measures did not stop the influx. According to Heer, it became apparent "that the legalization program for special agricultural workers was subject to considerable fraud,"[5] and when border agents caught people illegally sneaking into the United States, they merely sent them back across the border. The same people then snuck in again and again. In 1992, for example, immigration officers intercepted 12 million illegal immigrants from Mexico at the border, but they were simply sent home because the United States lacked enough jail space to accommodate them.

Mixed Reactions

Polls in the 1980s and 1990s indicated that many Americans felt that their communities were being overwhelmed even by legal immigrants. In a 1994 Pew Research Center poll, for example, 63 percent of Americans said immigrants were a burden to society because "they take our jobs, housing and health care,"[6] whereas 31 percent said immigrants strengthened the country because of their talents and hard work. During the late 20th century, a growing number of Americans also insisted that immigration should be stopped or slowed significantly. In 1966 a Gallup poll had indicated that 35 percent of Americans wanted immigration to decrease; in 1993 this number had increased to nearly 65 percent. Yet in 1990 the US government passed the Immigration Act of 1990, which increased the total number of immigrants allowed each year, expanded family-based and skills-based immigration, and created the diversity lottery program to allow fifty-five thousand immigrants from nations with historically few immigrants to America to be selected each year by a lottery system.

> "Americans have told pollsters long and loudly that they don't want any more immigration; but the politicians ignore them."[8]
>
> —Journalist Peter Brimelow

Public reaction to these changes was mixed. Immigration policy experts Faye Hipsman and Doris Meissner, for example, wrote that the huge number of immigrants that arrived in the 1990s "was an important element in achieving the productivity and prosperity of the decade."[7] Others, like journalist Peter Brimelow, noted, "Americans have told pollsters long and loudly that they don't want any more immigration; but the politicians ignore them."[8]

Immigrants' reasons for coming to the United States—"for riches, for land, for change, for tranquility, for freedom,"[9] according to American history professor Maldwyn Allen Jones—remained constant throughout American history, but debates about whether the time had come to close the immigration door became increasingly common during the 20th century. These debates spilled over into the 21st century as Americans' concerns about their own quality of life and about the ability of the government to control the US borders intensified with no resolution in sight.

Chapter Two

Did 20th-Century Immigration Harm the US Economy?

Immigration Harmed the US Economy

- Immigrants overwhelm taxpayer-funded programs.
- Immigrants strain school and health care budgets.
- Immigrants take American jobs and lower wages.

The Debate at a Glance

Immigration Helped the US Economy

- Immigrants have turned the United States into a global economic power.
- Immigrants raise wages and preserve businesses.
- Immigrants fill jobs Americans do not want.
- Immigrants contribute more than they cost America.

Immigration Harmed the US Economy

"Why allow even one unskilled worker into the country when we have so many of our own?"

—Cornell University labor economist Vernon M. Briggs Jr.

Vernon M. Briggs Jr., "Immigration and the U.S. Labor Market: Public Policy Gone Awry," Cornell University, ILR School, CAHRS Working Paper #92-41, October 1992. http://digitalcommons.ilr .cornell.edu.

Consider these questions as you read:

1. Do you believe that tax dollars should be reserved for needy US citizens rather than being used to assist needy immigrants? Why or why not?
2. What responsibilities should school districts have toward immigrant children who do not speak English and have a variety of other needs? Explain your answer.
3. What is your view of the claim that immigrants take jobs away from Americans?

Editor's note: The discussion that follows presents common arguments made in support of this perspective. All arguments are supported by facts, quotes, and examples taken from various sources of the period or present day.

Immigrants have adversely impacted the 20th-century American economy in a variety of ways. Many arrive in this country with little money and insufficient language skills to participate in the job market. They and their children, therefore, depend heavily on government-funded services for basic needs while contributing little to the overall economy.

Immigrants Overwhelm Taxpayer-Funded Programs

Many immigrants depend on publicly or privately funded charity to exist. After government welfare programs were implemented during the 1960s, immigrants were especially likely to depend on welfare and similar taxpayer-funded social services far more often than native-born Americans. This puts a burden on taxpayers and uses funds that are needed for American citizens.

Studies performed in New Jersey by researchers at Princeton University in 1989 and 1990 found that immigrant households in general impose a 46 percent higher economic burden on local, state, and federal government than do native-born households. The burden from Hispanic immigrant households is 60 percent higher. Most native-born households, in fact, are a net economic benefit to all three levels of government. This means that they contribute more in taxes to their local, state, and federal governments than they receive from government-funded welfare and other social services programs. The studies also found that "it is usually local governments that shoulder the most substantial burden in providing services to immigrant families."[10]

> "It is usually local governments that shoulder the most substantial burden in providing services to immigrant families."[10]
>
> —Princeton University study

California, which absorbed more immigrants than any other state between 1965 and 2000, is suffering particularly devastating economic consequences. A 1993 study by economist Donald Huddle found that the 7.2 million immigrants who came to California between 1970 and 1992 cost taxpayers $18.2 billion more in food stamps, welfare, free school lunches, and other programs than these immigrants paid in taxes. A separate study by demographics expert Michael Clune found that in 1995, Hispanic immigrants in Los Angeles County paid less in income and property taxes and received more in public assistance than any other group. Clune also found that one-third of the immigrants from Latin America had incomes below the poverty level and therefore received taxpayer-funded handouts for basic needs such as food and medical care.

The chain migration (families bringing in extended family members) that started in 1965 also threatens the taxpayer-funded Supplemental Security Income (SSI) program. SSI benefits are intended for Americans who are disabled or cannot work for other reasons. But immigrants who are not US citizens can receive SSI if they are related to someone who served in the US military; are disabled; are asylees or refugees; come from Cuba, Haiti, Amerasia, or certain other countries; or are victims of abuse. Meanwhile, Americans worry that SSI funds will not last long and that citizens who really need these funds may suffer.

Strained School and Health Care Budgets

Welfare-type benefits are not the only government programs that suffer because of immigration. Federal laws also require US municipalities and states to provide bilingual education and health care for immigrants. School districts nationwide are forced to spend increasing portions of their budgets on multilingual curricula, teachers, and related expenses, particularly in hard-hit states like California, Arizona, Michigan, and Texas. Demographic experts Leon Bouvier and John L. Martin say it costs 50 percent more to educate non-English-speaking children than English-speaking ones in the 1990s.

Not only do schools have to hire teachers who speak certain languages, but the hundreds of thousands of immigrant children also create overcrowded classrooms and the need for more schools. According to a study by the Rand research organization, in 1992 and 1993, New York City schools were overwhelmed with sixty-five thousand new immigrant children and experienced extremely overcrowded classrooms because there was no money to build the new schools the city needed. In California the number of new immigrants in the 1980s made officials realize they would need to build one new school every day to accommodate immigrant students, at a cost of around $15,000 per student. And immigrant children tend to be needier, and not just in terms of language skills; they require extra attention and services. For instance, some children come to the United States not even knowing what a pencil is—and the job of instructing these kids in pencil skills falls to teachers. The Rand study concludes, "The one common characteristic of most immigrant children is poverty," and since impoverished families pay little or no income taxes and pay no property taxes because they do not own their homes, the immigrants are obviously not contributing money to help educate their children. Thus, the study notes, "the [school] districts are profoundly troubled and are finding it difficult to provide sound educational experiences to any of their students."[11]

Federal laws that require hospitals to treat immigrants who cannot pay for their care have had similar economic effects. In 1993 and 1994, California spent $368 million on emergency medical care for illegal immigrants alone. In 1992 the state spent an additional $662.3 million on health and welfare benefits for the "anchor babies" whose mothers illegally cross the border to give birth in the United States so that their newborns will be American citizens entitled to government money. According to an article in the *Journal of American Physicians and Surgeons*, during the decade after 1994, eighty-four hospitals in California have had to shut down because they were swamped with illegals who paid nothing, and there was no room for paying patients. Even outspoken immigrant advocates like Linda Chavez, who directed the US Commission on Civil Rights in the 1990s, admitted in 1993 that these economic burdens must be addressed: "Yesteryear's 'huddled masses yearning to breathe free' were not thrust into the bosom of the welfare state. . . . We must curb both the abuses and anomalies of the current system."[12]

Immigrants Take Jobs and Lower Wages

Not only do immigrants use up public funds needed for American citizens, they also take citizens' jobs and lower their wages. To gain experience and earn income, many immigrants are willing to work for lower wages, which has a ripple effect in industries that employ large numbers of immigrants. Studies indicate that the mass immigrations since 1965 have been especially damaging for jobs and wages. Huddle found that in 1992 alone, immigrants displaced 914,000 workers in California from their jobs. Economist Thomas Muller and sociologist Thomas Espenshade found that large-scale Hispanic immigration to the Los Angeles area between 1970 and 1980 forced non-Hispanic whites, particularly those in low-skill jobs, to flee the city because the immigrants took their jobs. In fact, the non-Hispanic white population of Los Angeles County declined by 497,000 people between 1970 and 1980, whereas the population of Hispanic immigrants increased by 1.37 million. The Ameri-

> "Yesteryear's 'huddled masses yearning to breathe free' were not thrust into the bosom of the welfare state. . . . We must curb both the abuses and anomalies of the current system."[12]
>
> —Linda Chavez, former director of the US Commission on Civil Rights

can workers who stayed in the county reported that their wages plummeted because Hispanic immigrants were willing to work for lower wages.

Trade unions have objected loudly throughout the 20th century because many employers fired union members and hired immigrants who accepted lower wages than the unions demanded. In Los Angeles, for example, union-affiliated drywall installers who worked for housebuilders earned about $1,100 per week in the 1970s, and employers had to provide them with health insurance and pension funds. In the late 1970s housebuilders began hiring illegal Mexican laborers for around $300 per week with no benefits.

African Americans with low-skill jobs were especially hard-hit by the deluge of immigrants after 1965. A study by Richard Mines and Jeffrey Avina of Stanford University found that most of the African American union janitors in Los Angeles, who earned $12 per hour, lost their jobs between 1975 and 1985 because illegal Mexican and Central American immigrants accepted $4 per hour for janitorial work. Fifty-five thousand African Americans who worked in garment factories in Los Angeles in the 1970s also lost their jobs to immigrants.

In 1976 the INS estimated that between 6 million and 12 million illegal immigrants took jobs from Americans. When immigrant advocacy groups claimed that immigrants took hotel and restaurant jobs that Americans did not want, the INS produced data showing that at least 1 million illegal immigrants took blue- and white-collar jobs that many Americans did indeed want. Overall, because immigrants take jobs that Americans need, lower wages for many workers, and cost American taxpayers far more in social services and welfare programs than they contribute, the effects of immigration on the American economy are overwhelmingly negative.

Immigration Helped the US Economy

"Many Americans still believe that immigration hurts U.S. workers and the economy. Immigrants are perceived as taking jobs away from native-born Americans and filling the rolls for public assistance without paying their share of taxes to replenish the kitty. Nothing could be further from the truth."

—Economics writer Adam M. Zaretsky

Adam M. Zaretsky, "A Burden to America? Immigration and the Economy," Federal Reserve Bank of St. Louis, October 1997. www.stlouisfed.org.

Consider these questions as you read:

1. In your opinion what experiences and characteristics drive immigrants to strive for success in their adopted country?
2. Would you ever consider working as a janitor, maid, farmworker, dishwasher, gardener, or some other type of low-wage job? If so, under what conditions? If not, why not?
3. Do you agree with the argument that immigrants cost the country money when they first arrive, but they eventually give back to the economy far more than they take from it? Explain your answer.

Editor's note: The discussion that follows presents common arguments made in support of this perspective. All arguments are supported by facts, quotes, and examples taken from various sources of the period or present day.

Immigrants have helped the 20th-century American economy in many ways. For one thing their hard work has helped turn the United States into a global economic power. Influxes of immigrants have also raised overall wages in America and have preserved local businesses that might otherwise have moved overseas. In addition immigrants do many jobs Americans do not want to do, and they contribute billions of dollars to the US economy each year.

Immigrants Made the United States a Global Economic Power

The United States is an economic powerhouse thanks, in large part, to the hard work done by immigrants from many lands. Without these enterprising immigrants the country would have been much less likely to become the world's dominant economic power. As historian Maldwyn Allen Jones explains, immigrant labor and skills helped transform the United States "into a leading industrial power." Indeed, Jones states, "the realization of America's vast economic potential has . . . been due in significant measure to the efforts of immigrants."[13]

Most immigrants hope to forge a better and more prosperous life than they had in their home countries. Having little to lose and so much to gain, immigrants start new businesses, develop new technologies, and create opportunities for themselves and others. Men and women who fled Nazi oppression in Europe during the 1930s and 1940s, for instance, exemplify the economic and social contributions of immigrants. The scientific discoveries of Albert Einstein, for example, rocked the world of physics and were applied to new technologies, including nuclear energy. Later immigrants have also contributed to the US economy and to America's worldwide influence in shaping new technologies and other products. For example, Yahoo cofounder Jerry Yang (from Taiwan) and Google founder Sergey Brin (from Russia) pioneered many of the computer technologies that ushered in the world of the Internet. The growth of the companies they founded and the development of numerous other businesses related to their inventions have led to new jobs for many Americans and to widespread economic growth. As an article in the *Harvard Business Review* points out, "Technological innovation is a central

> "The realization of America's vast economic potential has . . . been due in significant measure to the efforts of immigrants."[13]
>
> —Historian Maldwyn Allen Jones

determinant of long-run economic growth, and access to the best inventors matters, regardless of their country of origin."[14]

Immigrants Raise Wages and Boost Business Activity

Even immigrants who work for others enhance the US economy. Immigration policy analyst David Bier has performed studies that show wages in the United States consistently rise during immigration waves. This is mostly because more immigrants mean more workers who can buy things, and more money flowing through the economy boosts the economic growth that drives wages upward. For example, Bier finds that between 1890 and 1914, when 15 million new immigrants arrived in the United States, wages rose 40 percent. In fact, the Ford Motor Company was able to pay automobile factory workers the highest wages in the world by 1914 because of economic growth fueled by the large number of immigrants who arrived in the United States between 1890 and 1914.

A study by economists Gianmarco Ottaviano and Giovanni Peri found that increased immigration to the United States has also increased wages during the late 20th century. The wage gains attributable to immigration have totaled between $30 billion and $80 billion per year between 1990 and the early 2000s and have benefited 90 percent of native-born workers. These facts led the president's Council of Economic Advisers to conclude that "immigration has a positive effect on the American economy as a whole and on the income of native-born American workers."[15]

In addition Bier's studies indicate that immigrants benefit native-born workers in another way—by helping these workers move to higher-level jobs. Bier found that by 1900, native-born Americans and previous generations of American immigrants occupied most of the skilled-labor positions, while new immigrants took lower-skilled positions. "By taking lower-skilled jobs, immigrants created better opportunities for Americans elsewhere in the economy,"[16] Bier explains.

Other studies indicate that even when immigrants depress wages for Americans in low-skill jobs, the lower wages allow manufacturers to hire more people and to expand production. During the last two decades of the 20th century, when many businesses have closed and/or moved their operations overseas to take advantage of cheaper labor, paying immigrants lower-than-normal wages has allowed many businesses to stay in the United States. According to sociology professor David Heer, lower wages "may preserve or expand certain industries in the United States that otherwise would not have survived foreign competition. Thus the lowering of wages for unskilled workers may create and make available to native workers new jobs as foremen, managers, professionals, and government workers that would not have existed otherwise."[17] One industry that hired many immigrants during the 1980s was the garment industry in cities like New York and Los Angeles. Garment factory owners faced with overseas competition realized that immigrants would work for $9 to $10 per day sewing clothing, whereas hiring unionized workers would cost about $5.50 per hour plus benefits. The lower wages kept these businesses profitable enough to stay in the United States.

> "The lowering of wages for unskilled workers may create and make available to native workers new jobs as foremen, managers, professionals, and government workers that would not have existed otherwise."[17]
>
> —Sociology professor David Heer

Immigrants Fill Jobs Americans Do Not Want

Besides having positive effects on wages and job prospects for American workers, immigrants help the economy by filling jobs that Americans do not want. New immigrants typically work in occupations such as gardening, housekeeping, farming, and meatpacking, as well as at low-skill jobs in factories and restaurants.

They fill vital positions that allow Americans to enjoy eating fresh fruits and vegetables, dining in restaurants, staying in hotels, having maids clean their houses, and many other activities—all at relatively low cost.

Numerous studies performed in the 1980s and 1990s quote employers who state that they cannot find native-born Americans to do low-skill jobs on farms and in factories and meatpacking plants. When they do hire native-born Americans, many state, these workers complain a lot and quit their jobs when asked to work hard. In contrast, immigrants have "a better work ethic . . .

Immigrants cut and package lettuce in Salinas, California. Unskilled immigrants often fill physically demanding and low-paying jobs that many Americans do not want, such as farming, gardening, and housekeeping.

work harder . . . are more diligent, punctual, persistent, reliable, respectful, and cooperative. . . . They act less 'entitled,'"[18] according to manufacturing supervisors. Indeed, most immigrants have sacrificed a great deal to come to the United States so it makes sense that they are willing to work hard.

Immigrants Contribute More to America than They Cost It

Like everyone else who lives in the United States, immigrants spend money and pay taxes. And the amounts they contribute to the economy in these ways are not insignificant. A study by the US Commission on Immigration Reform, for example, estimates that immigrants contributed between $1 billion and $10 billion to the US economy in the 1990s. Even when these contributions are contrasted with temporary help received from government welfare services, studies find immigrants still add a significant amount to the economy. During the late 20th century, for example, immigrants contributed $5 billion each year to the American economy while only receiving $1.1 billion in welfare and similar payments, says economist George Borjas. Immigrants' net contributions were therefore $4 billion each year.

To gain a truer picture of immigrant contributions to the economy, other economists look beyond day-to-day spending. They calculate future contributions. Once young immigrants complete their education, they become fully participating members of American society. Like their native-born counterparts, they work at jobs, start businesses, start families, buy houses and cars, take vacations, and contribute in all of the other usual ways to the nation's economy.

In many cases, though, the positive economic ramifications of immigration can be observed immediately. For example, during the late 20th century, immigrants were sparking new life in run-down inner-city neighborhoods throughout the country. As civil rights expert Linda Chavez explains, immigrants "have helped revitalize many urban neighborhoods and maintain a tax base in cities like New York and Los Angeles . . . [and thus] remain a tremendous national asset."[19] Indeed, in the late 1980s and early 1990s, about three hundred immigrants from Taiwan, Hong Kong, and Vietnam built up a deteriorating inner-city area of Los Angeles by establishing a thriving marketplace called Toy Town, in which they sold cheap toys from the Far East to toy retailers in the United States, Mexico, and Canada. In 1993 Toy Town employed about two thousand people.

The economic contributions immigrants make by starting businesses, filling essential jobs in agriculture and other industries, paying taxes, and spending money on goods and services are critical for growing and sustaining the US economy. Without immigrants America would soon lose its status as a world-class economic leader and powerhouse, and the quality of life for Americans would deteriorate. Immigrants are therefore an overwhelmingly positive economic force in the United States.

Chapter Three

Did 20th-Century Immigration Worsen Crime?

Immigration Worsened Crime

- Criminals are in the mix of immigrants arriving in America.
- Increased immigration leads to increased crime.
- Immigration provokes ethnic and racial violence.

The Debate at a Glance

Immigration Did Not Worsen Crime

- Immigrants commit fewer crimes than native-born Americans.
- Prejudice leads to misconceptions.
- Media hype is misleading.

Immigration Worsened Crime

"Our immigration policies are exacerbating our national epidemic of crime."

—Former Colorado governor Richard Lamm

Richard Lamm and Gary Imhoff, *The Immigration Time Bomb*. New York: Truman Talley, 1985, p. 49.

Consider these questions as you read:

1. What measures can or should the government take to ensure that people with criminal backgrounds do not immigrate to the United States?
2. Do concurrent increases in crime and in the number of immigrants prove that immigrants are responsible for increased crime rates, or might other factors be responsible? Explain your answer.
3. Do you agree with the statement that the presence of immigrants provokes ethnic and racial violence in American communities? Why or why not?

Editor's note: The discussion that follows presents common arguments made in support of this perspective. All arguments are supported by facts, quotes, and examples taken from various sources of the period or present day.

Anytime large numbers of people immigrate, there are bound to be criminals among them. And where there are criminals, there will also be crime. So although America prides itself on being a land of opportunity, it cannot allow people who have criminal connections and intentions to enter this country in hopes of becoming citizens. Too often, crime increases when large numbers of immigrants come to the United States.

Criminals in the Mix of Immigrants

It happened in the early 1900s when thousands of criminals, many with ties to the Italian Mafia, entered the United States with boatloads of other immigrants. Alarmed by the fact that these gangsters continued their criminal activities in America, Congress established the Dillingham Commission to investigate the impact of the large number of immigrants coming from Eastern and Southern Europe. In its 1911 report the Commission concluded that "the coming of criminals and persons of criminal tendencies constitutes one of the serious social effects of the immigration movement." It specifically noted the threat posed by immigrants from Eastern and Southern Europe. Even though federal law prohibits "the diseased, defective, delinquent, and dependent"[20] from immigrating, the Commission pointed out, officials were powerless to prevent criminals from misrepresenting themselves and sneaking aboard ships bearing hundreds of immigrants. This unfortunate reality stemmed from the fact that shipping agents in immigrants' countries of origin and American inspectors had no foolproof method of identifying undesirable people.

Mobsters who emigrated from Sicily in southern Italy set up numerous types of criminal enterprises that involved bribery, theft, murder, and other crimes. "By the 1920s, petty extortion had escalated in urban areas, and underworld crime had become big business,"[21] explain the authors of the book *Liberty, Equality, Power*. The Mafia established profitable, but illegal, prostitution, liquor, and gambling businesses. They also threatened owners of small and medium-sized businesses with violence or economic ruin unless they paid Mafia mobsters for "protection" from criminals. Mafia team members known as enforcers then beat up or killed those who did not comply with these extortion

> "By the 1920s, petty extortion had escalated in urban areas, and underworld crime had become big business."[21]
>
> —The authors of the book *Liberty, Equality, Power*

demands. One of the most notorious mobsters was Al Capone, who earned millions of dollars through his prostitution, gambling, and bootleg liquor businesses and had scores of people killed.

Organized crime and independent immigrant criminals also routinely bribed government officials. Businesses run by immigrants from Ireland, Italy, and other countries were eager to win contracts to install city services like sewer and trolley systems. They paid off government officials in charge of these matters in exchange for contracts. These criminals also curried political favors by setting up political machines—illegal organizations that made sure certain politicians won elections. Political machine bosses either paid local voters to vote for their candidates or bribed these voters by promising to find people jobs in exchange for votes. The Irish ancestors of President John F. Kennedy were prominent examples of political machine bosses in Boston. Kennedy's grandfathers, John Francis Fitzgerald and Patrick Joseph Kennedy, traded jobs and cash for votes that favored certain Irish Democrats in the early 1900s.

In the early 1900s thousands of criminals with ties to the Italian Mafia entered the United States along with boatloads of other immigrants. In the 1920s, Al Capone (pictured) became one of the most powerful Mafia mobsters in history.

Foreign Governments Export Criminals

The mobsters and other criminals that came to the United States among other immigrants did plenty of damage, but instances in which foreign governments deliberately exported dangerous criminals are even more alarming. In 1980 Cuba dumped nearly three thousand criminals and people with mental illnesses on the United States in what is known as the Mariel boatlift. It was orchestrated by Cuban Americans in Florida and Cuban dictator Fidel Castro. Castro announced that Cubans who wanted to immigrate to the United States could board boats at the port in Mariel, starting on April 20, 1980. Between April and October, 125,000 Cubans arrived in Florida on seventeen hundred overloaded boats, overwhelming the US Coast Guard and officials in the Miami area. The US government soon discovered that among the immigrants were more than twenty-seven hundred violent criminals and people with mental illnesses that Cuban authorities had released from prisons and mental hospitals.

Some of the Cuban criminals were deported, but since neither Cuba nor any other country would take most of them, many remained

> "The hardened criminals among the boat people did not change their ways, and their criminal activities generated a crime wave in Florida."[22]
>
> —Deputy US Secretary of State John A. Bushnell

in US jails. Others roamed free on American soil until they committed heinous crimes here in their adopted home. Among those, Julio Gonzalez was later convicted of arson and murder after starting the Happy Land fire at the Happy Land Social Club in Bronx, New York, on March 25, 1990; Luis Felipe founded the New York branch of the Latin Kings gang; Pedro Medina was executed in Florida in 1997 for murdering a woman; and Jesus Mezquia murdered punk rock singer Mia Zapata in 1993. Most of the Mariel criminals remained in Florida. According to John A. Bushnell, the deputy US secretary of state in 1980, "The hardened criminals among the boat people did not change their ways, and their criminal activities generated a crime wave in Florida."[22]

Increased Immigration Leads to Increased Violent Crime

One could argue that anecdotes like these are not proof that crime increases with immigration. However, other evidence exists. Studies show a clear connection between waves of immigration and vast increases in violent crime. Jeffrey S. Adler, a professor of history and criminology, notes that the homicide, robbery-homicide, and robbery rates in the United States increased by almost 50 percent between 1900 and 1925. This was especially evident in cities with large immigrant populations, such as Baltimore, Chicago, and New York. The increase in crime corresponded with the arrival of about 18 million new immigrants.

Further corroboration for the link between immigrants and crime comes from evidence that crime rates and immigration rates both decreased dramatically between the mid-1920s and 1940. The homicide and robbery-homicide rates declined by more than 40 percent between 1921 and 1940. At the same time the US census shows that the number of immigrants decreased to about 4.6 million compared to 14.5 million between 1901 and 1920.

In the decades that followed, immigrants continued to commit a disproportionate number of crimes. One study found that immigrants committed 83 percent of the crimes in Smyrna, Georgia, in the 1990s. Additionally, the 1991 Survey of State Prisons found that a disproportionately high percentage of inmates in state prisons were immigrants. Forty-seven percent of these immigrants were from Mexico, and another 26 percent were from South American or Caribbean countries. Surveys of US federal prisons yielded similar results; in 1994 more than 70 percent of the inmates were identified as immigrants from Latin America. In general, during the 1990s, immigrants from Cuba and the Dominican Republic were incarcerated four to five times more frequently than US citizens; and immigrants from Mexico, Jamaica, and Colombia were incarcerated two to two-and-one-half times more frequently.

Immigrant Presence Provokes
Ethnic and Racial Violence

Immigrants do not just commit more crimes than Americans; their presence also incites racial and ethnic violence. Immigrant-fueled violence occurred in the 1920s and 1930s in Salt Lake River, Arizona, where white farmers were incensed that Japanese immigrants bought up prime land and successfully farmed and sold fruits and vegetables. During the Great Depression, in 1934, the white farmers told the Japanese farmers to leave because they were preventing native-born Americans from earning a living. The immigrants refused, and the white farmers vowed to "protect our homes and livelihood from the law-breaking alien."[23] They began attacking Japanese property and people; this even created a diplomatic crisis between the US and Japanese governments.

Another example of immigrant-fueled violence occurred in Los Angeles in April and May 1992. Thousands of African Americans rioted to express their displeasure over the acquittal of four police officers who beat a black man named Rodney King. These rioters specifically targeted Korean and Hispanic immigrant shop owners because they resented the fact that immigrants stole their jobs and pushed them out of neighborhoods that became ethnic enclaves. Police ended up arresting about twelve thousand African American rioters.

Another factor that fueled resentment toward Korean immigrants in Los Angeles was that Korean shopkeepers often accused blacks of shoplifting. In one case in 1991, a Korean shopkeeper killed a black teenaged girl after she stole merchandise and hit the shopkeeper. Korean immigrants armed themselves with guns after local police refused to protect them. Anger among blacks led to retaliatory violence during the 1992 riots and on other occasions during the 1990s.

Clearly, immigrants are responsible for increasing crime in America. Sometimes the immigrants themselves commit a variety of crimes, and other times their presence drives others to break the law. Either way, lawlessness and immigrants go hand in hand.

Immigration Did Not Worsen Crime

"There is no consistent or compelling evidence . . . that immigration causes crime."

—Law professor John Hagan and sociologist Alberto Palloni

Quoted in National Research Council, *The Immigration Debate: Studies on the Economic, Demographic, and Fiscal Effects of Immigration*. Washington, DC: National Academies Press, 1998, p. 380.

Consider these questions as you read:

1. Why do you think many Americans throughout the 20th century accused immigrants of having criminal tendencies even when statistics showed otherwise?
2. In your view how much power do politicians and the news media have in swaying public opinion—and why does this matter?
3. When native-born Americans accuse immigrants of adding to the crime rate, do these accusations reflect characteristics of the immigrants or of the native-born Americans? Explain your reasoning.

Editor's note: The discussion that follows presents common arguments made in support of this perspective. All arguments are supported by facts, quotes, and examples taken from various sources of the period or present day.

The assertion that immigrants increase crime is false. Countless studies and congressional commissions' research show that immigrants committed fewer crimes than native-born Americans during the 20th century. Widespread perceptions that immigrants import crime result from prejudice and from media hype about isolated incidents.

Immigrants Commit Fewer Crimes than Native-Born Americans

Numerous studies show that immigrants are less likely than native-born Americans to commit crimes. Sociologist Bianca Bersani and criminologist Alex Piquero studied crime reports, prison records, and research reports from the 20th century to determine whether immigrants committed more crimes than native-born Americans. In their report they conclude, "Research dating back more than a century documents a pattern whereby the foreign-born are involved in crime at significantly lower rates than their peers."[24]

Bersani and Piquero also note that investigations during every part of the 1900s confirmed that commonly held views about immigrant criminality were mistaken. For example, in 1931, the congressional Wickersham Commission reported that "in proportion to their respective numbers the foreign born commit considerably fewer crimes than the native born."[25] Later on, analyses of US census data from 1980 to 2000 showed that native-born men aged eighteen to forty-nine were five times more likely to be incarcerated than immigrant men in this age group. A study by researchers at the University of California, San Francisco, and the University of North Carolina at Chapel Hill also found that foreign-born youth in American middle and high schools in the 1990s had lower delinquency rates than native-born students.

> "Research dating back more than a century documents a pattern whereby the foreign-born are involved in crime at significantly lower rates than their peers."[24]
>
> —Sociologist Bianca Bersani and criminologist Alex Piquero

Why the Lower Crime Rates?

Sociologist Robert Sampson's research sheds light on factors that influence immigrants' lower rates of violent crime. Sampson

Studies have shown that violent crime rates in the 1990s in Chicago were lower among Mexican immigrants than native-born Americans. Strong family connections among Mexicans is considered a strong deterrent to involvement in crime.

compared rates of violent crime among Mexican immigrants and native-born Americans in the 1990s in Chicago. He found that Mexican immigrants committed fewer violent crimes than native-born Americans. He attributes the lower rate of violence among Mexican immigrants to a combination of factors including stable family life, which is considered a strong deterrent to involvement in crime.

Studies by sociologists also reveal that immigrants have a positive effect on overall crime rates. Sociologist Tim Wadsworth writes that the drop in homicides and robberies during the 1990s was at least partly due to immigration: "Cities with the largest increase in immigration between 1990 and 2000 experienced the largest decreases in homicide and robbery during the same time period. . . . Growth in immigration may have been responsible for part of the precipitous crime drop of the 1990s."[26] Wadsworth is unsure of the reasons for this but suggests that the close-knit families and traditional values that are common in immigrant households might be a factor.

Prejudice Leads to Misconceptions

The evidence that proves immigrants commit fewer crimes than native-born Americans is strong, but many Americans are blinded to this reality by their own biases. In some cases Americans wrongly assume that all immigrants broke the law to enter or remain in the United States and are thus criminals. For instance, a 1993 *Time* magazine survey found that nearly two-thirds of Americans believe most immigrants enter the United States illegally, when, in fact, most enter the country legally. In fact, the US government estimates that about 300,000 illegal immigrants entered the United States in 1990, compared to 1.8 million legal immigrants.

In other cases public officials encourage prejudice—and thus nurture misconceptions—by referring to all immigrants as criminals. In 1912, for example, the superintendent of New York state prisons portrayed immigrants as a blight upon the state. He said, "A large proportion of the vicious and ignorant . . . make the large cities their headquarters. Thus there is forced upon New York State and upon its charitable and penal institutions more than their due proportion of the undesirable classes of immigrants: the lawless, the illiterate, and the defective."[27] Likewise, in 1916, the American Bar Association blamed immigrants for the nation's crime woes and argued for a slowing of immigration. The organization wrote that "the volume of crime in the United States is disproportionately increased by immigration, and that, in consequence to reduce crime, immigration must be reduced."[28]

These and similar comments fueled American distrust of immigrants and magnified the mistaken notion that most immigrants were criminals. Lost in all the hysteria were the findings of the Dillingham Commission, which Congress appointed in 1907 to study the effects of immigration on society. The commission's 1911 report assured the public that "immigration has not increased the volume of crime."[29] It further stated that immigrants may have even suppressed criminal activity. But these findings were largely ignored.

In 1931 the Wickersham Commission set up by Congress to investigate the criminal justice system also concluded that immigrants commit fewer crimes than native-born Americans. Its finding was based on extensive surveys of crime and prison records nationwide. However, many Americans continued to believe that immigrants were responsible for most of the criminal activities in the country. In 1933 criminologist Donald R. Taft alluded to the Wickersham report when he stated that "the popular view of the role of the immigrant in crime is grossly exaggerated if not altogether erroneous."[30]

> "Few stereotypes of immigrants are as enduring, or have been proven so categorically false over literally decades of research, as the notion that immigrants are disproportionately likely to engage in criminal activity."[31]
>
> —The Carnegie Endowment for International Peace and the Urban Institute

In 1997 a study commissioned by the Carnegie Endowment for International Peace and the Urban Institute made a similar observation about prejudice: "Few stereotypes of immigrants are as enduring, or have been proven so categorically false over literally decades of research, as the notion that immigrants are disproportionately likely to engage in criminal activity."[31]

Media Hype Is Misleading

Closely related to this widespread prejudice is the fact that anti-immigrationists and the media deliberately hype criminal acts by immigrants to make it seem like all immigrants or all immigrants of a particular nationality or ethnicity are criminals. For example, in the early to mid-20th century, news stories about Italian and Jewish gangsters, such as Al Capone and Meyer Lansky, got prominent play in newspapers across the country. These reports contributed to the belief by members of the public that all Italian and Jewish immigrants were criminals.

Although gangsters constituted a tiny minority of these immigrants, hostility toward them grew. Historians report that violence due to prejudice against immigrant Jews was especially prevalent in New York City and Boston, where gangs of Irish youths routinely attacked Jews and vandalized Jewish homes. Media-hyped stories about Italian mobsters also led to violence against Italians; one study documented nearly fifty lynchings of Italians nationwide between 1890 and 1920. In one lynching in New Orleans, a mob of people killed eleven Italians who they believed were responsible for killing a police officer. Afterward numerous newspaper articles stated that the lynching was an appropriate way to deal with Italians because Italians were genetically prone to violence.

In the 1920s the *Chicago Tribune* newspaper hyped gangster-related crimes in its stories and headlines. For instance, the newspaper prominently displayed this quote by the president of the Chicago Crime Commission: "The real Americans are not gangsters. Recent immigrants and the first generation of Jews and Italians are the chief offenders, with the Jews furnishing the brains and the Italians the brawn."[32]

Similar hype and misinformation occurred during later decades of the 20th century. In 1951, for example, President Harry Truman's Commission on Migratory Labor issued a report that blamed low wages and social ills on illegal immigrants and called the increasing number of illegals "virtually an invasion."[33] In 1943 Los Angeles radio announcer B. Tarkington Dowlen called for the US government to deport the 500,000 Mexican farmworkers in Southern California because they were "inherently dishonest," and 70 percent of them were "afflicted with syphilis."[34]

This type of media hype not only promoted widespread prejudice but it also led to public approval of harassment and deportation of Latino immigrants. For instance, in 1954 the public supported a large-scale roundup and deportation of Mexican immigrants in California known as Operation Wetback. (*Wetback* is a disparaging term used to describe Mexicans who swim across the Rio Grande on the US border.) Military troops, border patrol agents, and state police swept through Mexican immigrant communities and loaded residents (regardless of their legal status or citizenship) into large trucks that took them to detention centers near the border. Aircraft, trains, trucks, or boats then transported these individuals to southern Mexico to make it difficult for them to quickly recross the border.

Throughout the 20th century, media-fanned prejudice against immigrants of all races, ethnicities, and nationalities has strongly influenced the public's perception that all immigrants have criminal tendencies. Yet study after study has confirmed that immigrants are less likely than native-born Americans to be involved in criminal activities. The logical conclusion is that immigration does not worsen crime in the United States.

Chapter Four

Did 20th-Century Immigration Threaten American Culture?

Immigration Threatened American Culture

- Immigrants are unwilling to abandon their old culture and traditions and adopt new ones.
- Immigrants dilute standards of American excellence.
- In their own communities native-born Americans find themselves in a foreign world.

The Debate at a Glance

Immigration Did Not Threaten American Culture

- American culture is unique because of its diversity.
- Immigrants share a commitment to American values.
- Immigrants enhance American culture.

Immigration Threatened American Culture

"Major cities have already been turned into extensions of foreign countries. Aliens threaten to seize political power within a few short years."

—Gordon McDonald, former US Border Patrol chief

Quoted in Hoover Institution, "Immigration and the Rise and Decline of American Cities," August 1, 1997. www.hoover.org.

Consider these questions as you read:

1. Do you think bilingual or multilingual education damages American cultural unity? Why or why not?
2. Do you agree or disagree with claims that immigrants who cling to their ancestral cultures have destroyed America's reputation for excellence? Explain your reasoning.
3. What do you think about assertions by some native-born Americans that 20th-century immigrants have turned America into an unfamiliar, foreign place, and, in this way, have threatened its future?

Editor's note: The discussion that follows presents common arguments made in support of this perspective. All arguments are supported by facts, quotes, and examples taken from various sources of the period or present day.

Immigration is not just a process by which someone changes his or her country of residence. In the United States, at least, it has traditionally been a process that involves adopting a new way of life. This means embracing the cultural traditions, customs, and values of one's new home. Too many immigrants in the 20th century have rejected this view of immigration—and in the process are threatening the American way of life.

Immigrants Hold On to Their Old Cultures

Immigrants threaten American culture and values because they are unwilling to abandon their old culture and traditions and adopt new ones. Social scientists note that a nation's culture derives from shared morals, values, language, and basic goals. Political scientist Samuel P. Huntington, for example, describes America's core culture as "primarily the culture of the seventeenth- and eighteenth-century settlers who founded American society . . . [including] the Christian religion, Protestant values and moralism, a work ethic, the English language, British traditions of law, justice, and the limits of government power, and a legacy of European art, literature, philosophy, and music."[35]

When immigrants express a desire to live with their own kind, speak their native language, and hang on to old customs, this threatens US stability. When immigrants settle in ethnic enclaves and wave the flag of their native lands during public events, they identify themselves as what President Theodore Roosevelt called hyphenated Americans. In his 1915 speech dubbed the "Unhyphenated America" speech, Roosevelt explained how allegiance to non-American cultures weakens the United States:

> "The one absolutely certain way of bringing this nation to ruin, of preventing all possibility of its continuing to be a nation at all, would be to permit it to become a tangle of squabbling nationalities . . . each preserving its separate nationality."[36]
>
> —President Theodore Roosevelt in 1915

A hyphenated American is not an American at all. . . . Our allegiance must be purely to the United States. . . . The one absolutely certain way of bringing this nation to ruin, of preventing all possibility of its continuing to be a nation at all, would be to permit it to become a tangle of squabbling nationalities, an intricate knot of German-Americans,

Irish-Americans, English-Americans, French-Americans, Scandinavian-Americans or Italian-Americans, each preserving its separate nationality.[36]

The threats to American culture have intensified as the 20th century progresses and more and more immigrants refuse to let go of the old and accept the new. According to historian, educator, and public official Arthur M. Schlesinger Jr., immigrants' unwillingness to adopt American culture has created lasting di-

In 1915 President Theodore Roosevelt (pictured) explained how immigrants' allegiance to non-American cultures weakens the United States. He referred to such immigrants as "hyphenated Americans."

visiveness: "A cult of ethnicity has arisen both among non-Anglo whites and among nonwhite minorities to denounce the goal of assimilation, to challenge the concept of 'one people' and to protect, promote, and perpetuate separate ethnic and racial communities. . . . [This] nourishes prejudices, magnifies differences, and stirs antagonisms."[37]

Immigrants' Demands Divide America

When the immigration floodgates opened in 1965, immigrants (particularly those from Mexico) started demanding bilingual education. Although the original stated intent was to help immigrant children learn English, by 1985 bilingual education was viewed as "a way of enhancing students' knowledge of their native language and culture . . . an emblem of cultural pride,"[38] according to Huntington. This makes it especially damaging to American cultural unity.

The language battles are especially contentious since, as Huntington states, "Throughout American history English has been central to American national identity. . . . Without a common language, communication becomes difficult if not impossible, and the nation becomes the arena for two or more language communities."[39]

> "How much 'diversity' can we tolerate before we cease to be one nation and one people?"[40]
>
> —Journalist and political activist Patrick J. Buchanan

The result is a divided society. One study in San Diego in the 1990s found that bilingual education and multiculturalism squelched immigrant children's identification as Americans to the point that more than 50 percent of Mexican immigrants identified themselves as Mexican. In 1997 journalist and political activist Patrick J. Buchanan framed the issue by asking, "How much 'diversity' can we tolerate before we cease to be one nation and one people?"[40]

Immigrants Defeat American Excellence

In addition to dividing and weakening American culture, 20th-century immigrants have also destroyed America's status as a country that promotes excellence and leads the way in education, business, the arts, and sciences. The international community began noticing the deterioration of American excellence as immigration levels increased dramatically during the last three decades of the 20th century. "At a time when attention is directed to the general decline in American exceptionalism, American immigration continues to flow at a rate unknown elsewhere in the rest of the world,"[41] a team of international social scientists concluded in a study done in the late 1980s.

Immigrants who reject American culture and instead hold on to the standards of living and cultural practices of their countries of origin threaten to dilute America's own standards of excellence. Instead of considering mastery of English composition, US history, math, and so on to be the standards to which their children should aspire, immigrants demand that public schools teach students about their native cultures. According to commentator Stephen Webster, along with the focus on elevating the importance of other cultures comes an emphasis on villainizing traditional American culture as racist and exclusionary. Webster notes that with these assaults on American culture, "immigration is destroying the unity and cultural coherence of the country."[42]

Sociologist James Davison Hunter notes that villainizing traditional American culture and values is confusing for everyone, especially for American children, who start to think that the values represented by their own culture lack authority and validity. "Multiculturalists wish to increase the recognition, power, and legitimacy of various minority groups, in part through a de-legitimation of an oppressive mainstream American culture," Hunter writes. The result is that "multiculturalism undermines the authority of cultural norms and cultural institutions."[43]

With so many new immigrants, schools are having trouble—not just keeping up but also maintaining high educational standards. In 1988 only 5 percent of American high school students could read well enough to understand college-level books. SAT scores fell 41 percent between 1972 and 1991. Experts largely attribute these declines to overcrowding by non-English-speaking immigrants. Author Spencer P. Morrison, for instance, who often writes about immigration issues, notes that public schools, particularly in California and Texas, are suffering the effects of large class sizes and insufficient funds. "Schools must spend time on remedial lessons and hire expensive translators, rather than helping students get ahead,"[44] says Morrison. Indeed, teachers are told to focus on helping non-English-speaking children who drag down the level of learning for everyone.

Americans Find Themselves in a Foreign World

In addition to weakening American culture and standards of excellence, rising numbers of immigrants in the 20th century drastically changed demographics and made native-born Americans feel like outsiders in their own country. In 1970 whites made up 85 percent of the American population. By 1995 this number dropped to 75 percent because of huge numbers of nonwhite immigrants and their high birth rates. As foreigners cluster in ethnic enclaves where foreign languages are spoken and displayed on storefronts and foreign cultural traditions are observed, more and more Americans feel like once-familiar places are now foreign countries. "It is difficult to explain to residents of the community that the Indo-Chinese refugees are drying skinned cats out on the clothes line because they enjoy cats as a delicacy in their country,"[45] the mayor of Santa Ana, California, told a congressional committee in 1981.

Millions of native-born Americans flee from areas that seem like foreign countries. In California, which absorbed a large number of immigrants throughout the 20th century, 2 million native-born Californians moved to Nevada, Arizona, Colorado, Idaho, and other states in the 1990s "to live out their lives in places more like the Golden State they grew up in,"[46] according to Buchanan. Something similar has happened in Atlanta, Georgia, where developers built new suburban communities for the large number of native-born Americans—both white and black—who have left neighborhoods that no longer feel like home.

Buchanan is one of many political commentators who predict that these demographic changes threaten the very existence of America. "America faces an existential crisis," Buchanan writes in his book *State of Emergency*. "If we do not get control of our borders, by 2050 Americans of European descent will be a minority in the nation their ancestors created and built. No nation has ever undergone so radical a demographic transformation and survived."[47]

By taking over neighborhoods and entire cities, by denigrating traditional American culture, and by replacing American standards of excellence with their own standards, 20th-century immigrants weaken American cultural unity and increase the number of Americans who feel out of place in their own country. It is therefore accurate to conclude that immigrants are a huge threat to American culture and values.

Immigration Did Not Threaten American Culture

"America has always been an open, fluid, commercial culture. It has embraced those willing to play the game its way, and today's immigrants are as willing to do so as any of their predecessors have been."

—Writer James Fallows

James Fallows, "Immigration: How It's Affecting Us," *Atlantic*, November 1983. www.the atlantic.com.

Consider these questions as you read:

1. Do you believe that the United States is a melting pot? Why or why not?
2. How would you describe the term *assimilation*, and how important is assimilation in a country such as the United States? Explain your reasoning.
3. Do you believe it is possible for immigrants to assimilate into American society while at the same time retaining their home country's customs and traditions? Why or why not?

Editor's note: The discussion that follows presents common arguments made in support of this perspective. All arguments are supported by facts, quotes, and examples taken from various sources of the period or present day.

The United States has a unique history and culture. One of the things that makes this country so special is its immigrant past and present. People have come to America from countries around the globe. In so doing they have brought with them a rich variety of cultural traditions and values that have, over time, blended to create a unique American culture and way of life. Far from threatening that culture and way of life, immigrants are its foundation.

American Culture Is Unique

The motto of the United States, "E Pluribus Unum," which appears on the great seal designed in the late 1700s, exemplifies the uniqueness of America. The translation, "Out of many, one,"[48] refers to uniting the original thirteen colonies and bringing together immigrants from diverse countries into one nation. That tradition continues today.

Unlike the United States, the populations of the world's other countries consist primarily of one dominant people and culture. When immigrants come to those countries, they are expected to abandon their old customs and values and adopt the dominant culture. America, on the other hand, consists of people from many parts of the world who have many different backgrounds. Immigrants have always added the rich traditions and customs of their home countries to the unique mix that is the American culture and way of life. Hector St. John de Crèvecoeur, a Frenchman who immigrated to America in 1759, described his adopted home as a place where immigrants "melted into a new race of men . . . [and became] a new man, who acts upon new principles."[49] This idea of the United States as a melting pot continued to define the American way of life throughout much of the 20th century.

> "E Pluribus Unum . . . out of many, one."[48]
>
> —The motto of the United States

In 1958 John F. Kennedy, who later became the thirty-fifth president of the United States, wrote the book *A Nation of Immigrants*. In his book, Kennedy describes how diverse cultural traditions have merged into and enriched a distinctively American culture. He uses food as one example. "One writer," he states, "has suggested that a 'typical American menu' might include some of the following dishes: 'Irish stew, chop suey, goulash, chile con carne, ravioli, knockwurst mit sauerkraut, Yorkshire pudding, Welsh rarebit, borscht, gefilte fish, Spanish omelette, caviar, mayonnaise, antipasto, baumkuchen, English muffins, gruyère cheese, Danish pastry, Canadian bacon, hot tamales, wiener-schnitzel, petit fours, spumoni, bouillabaisse, mate, scones, Turkish coffee, minestrone, filet mignon."[50]

The imagery of America as a melting pot was later revised. At one point, the favored metaphor was a salad bowl. Historian Carl Degler suggested the salad bowl metaphor in the 1950s. Degler noted that many immigrants and their descendants retain their original cultural traditions. "A more accurate analogy," he writes, "would be a salad bowl, for although the salad is an entity, the lettuce can still be distinguished from the chicory, the tomatoes from the cabbage."[51] Regardless of which metaphor is used, people throughout the world agree that the unique blend of cultural traditions in America enhance, rather than threaten, American culture.

Immigrants Share a Commitment to American Values

Aside from enriching American culture and way of life, immigrants have shown their devotion to the country's core principles of democracy, liberty, and opportunity. Many immigrants have, in fact, escaped societies in which democracy, liberty, and opportunity simply do not or did not exist. Cuba and the former Soviet Union are well-known examples. Immigrants from countries like these, therefore, have a strong appreciation for those values that are the foundation of American life. And most are determined to not only adopt those values but to also see that their children adopt them and benefit from them.

If there is one thing that Americans from all walks of life value, it is hard work. And when it comes to hard work, immigrants are usually at the top. Many leave behind friends, family, and established careers. When they arrive, they are often unfamiliar with American customs and have limited knowledge of English. The transition to becoming an American can be exceedingly difficult, but immigrants continually demonstrate both willingness and ability to make this happen—if not for themselves, then at least for their children and their grandchildren. As sociologist Charles

Hirschman writes, "Almost by definition, immigrants are risk-takers. . . . Most have traveled long distances, faced bureaucratic barriers and have sometimes even risked life and limb to reach their destinations. These characteristics mean that they will not be easily deterred from their goals."[52]

Immigrants Embrace US Culture

What Americans who are long removed from the immigrant experience often forget or fail to acknowledge is how difficult immigration can be. Many new immigrants, overwhelmed by the newness and unfamiliarity of their new home, cling to familiar customs and language and live among earlier immigrants from their home countries. This pattern can be seen throughout the 20th century in the Germantowns, Chinatowns, Little Italys, and other ethnic neighborhoods that have sprouted around the country. But sometimes it just takes time for these individuals to feel comfortable enough with American life that they are ready to incorporate American cultural practices into their lifestyles. In other cases first-generation immigrants never fully assimilate. However, even when this happens, successive generations assimilate more readily. One Pew Research Center study shows that 90 percent of second-generation Hispanic and Asian immigrants speak English well, and about 60 percent call themselves "a typical American," compared to about 30 percent of first-generation immigrants. Second-generation Hispanic and Asian immigrants are also far more likely to have friends outside their ethnic group and to marry

> "Immigrants are risk-takers. . . . Most have traveled long distances, faced bureaucratic barriers and have sometimes even risked life and limb to reach their destinations. These characteristics mean that they will not be easily deterred from their goals."[52]
>
> —Sociologist Charles Hirschman

Chinatown in New York City attracts both Chinese and non-Chinese Americans and tourists. Ethnic neighborhoods, including Chinatowns and Little Italys, developed around the country as incoming immigrants longed for familiar customs in America.

outside this group. At the same time, according to the Pew study, "Most in the second generation also have a strong sense of identity with their ancestral roots."[53] This allows them to retain their cultural traditions while at the same time embracing and adopting American culture as their own.

Immigrant Contributions

Immigrants do not merely blend the cultures of their native lands with American culture; their multicultural perspective helps them greatly enrich American culture in new ways. As Hirschman notes, being reared in multiple cultures gives immigrants "multiple frames of reference; they can see more choices, possibilities, interpretations, and nuance than persons who are familiar with only one culture. . . . [This can] stimulate creativity [and] greater openness to innovation."[54]

Musician Al Jolson is an example of an immigrant who forged new cultural ground during the 20th century. Jolson arrived with his family as a Russian Jewish immigrant child named Asa Yoelson in the late 1880s. Asa's beautiful singing voice led his family to assume he would succeed his father as a cantor in a synagogue. But Asa wanted to be a pop singer. He changed his name and left home to create his vision of a new musical style known as jazz. By the 1920s Jolson was one of the most famous American entertainers. But as Hirschman explains, Jolson was more than an immigrant who made a name for himself. Jolson redefined "the role and image of a public performer" by introducing stage runways and delivering emotional performances unlike any ever seen before. "The Jolson style did not represent assimilation, but rather the creation of a distinctive 'American' genre of musical performance"[55] that influenced later performers, Hirschman contends, including Bing Crosby, Judy Garland, and Neil Diamond.

Other immigrants who changed and enriched American culture include movie producer and Italian immigrant Frank Capra, who directed *It's a Wonderful Life* and *Mr. Smith Goes to Washington* in the 1930s and 1940s. This launched an era of films that celebrated average Americans and small-town life. And when Russian immigrant George Balanchine founded the New York City Ballet in 1948, he pioneered a new style of uniquely American dance that differed from the usual European-influenced dance styles.

With all that immigrants do to enrich American culture, and because they share basic American values, it is apparent that they do not threaten American culture and values. Instead, immigrants help to continuously infuse new life and new perspectives into the ever-evolving country whose culture was and is built on the contributions of diverse individuals from diverse places.

Chapter Five

Did 20th-Century America Have Room for New Immigrants?

America Had Plenty of Room for New Immigrants

- Fear, not facts, drives anti-immigration sentiment.
- Immigrants revitalize America.
- Immigrants are needed to fill jobs and maintain a vibrant economy.

The Debate at a Glance

America Had No Room for New Immigrants

- America is too crowded.
- Immigrants worsen environmental damage.
- Americans favor less or no immigration.

America Had Plenty of Room for New Immigrants

"Surely the United States at the end of the twentieth century is resourceful enough to deal with an immigrant inflow proportionally half what American society managed to deal with quite successfully in the early years of this century."

—Historian David M. Kennedy

David M. Kennedy, "Can We Still Afford to Be a Nation of Immigrants?," *Atlantic*, November 1996. www.theatlantic.com.

Consider these questions as you read:

1. Do you believe that the United States has room for more immigrants? Why or why not?
2. What can happen when people make decisions and judgments based on fear rather than facts?
3. Is the need to keep the population growing and vibrant a valid reason to encourage more immigration? Why or why not?

Editor's note: The discussion that follows presents common arguments made in support of this perspective. All arguments are supported by facts, quotes, and examples taken from various sources of the period or present day.

The notion that there is no more room for immigrants in America is based on fear rather than fact. Many native-born Americans fear immigrants' diversity and their negative effects on America's economy and culture. But facts prove that immigrants are needed now more than ever because they contribute positively to many aspects of American life. Immigrants built up America in its early days, and they have continued to revitalize the nation throughout the 20th century.

Fear Versus Fact

The argument that the United States already has too many immigrants and should not accept more is based on fears about overcrowding, unfamiliar cultures, and changing demographics. America is a huge country, and in the 18th, 19th, and early 20th centuries there was plenty of room for more people. Yet consider the following quote related to fears about new immigrants crowding out native-born Americans and corrupting American culture: "Few of their children in the country learn English. . . . The signs in our streets have inscriptions in both languages. . . . Unless the stream of the importation could be turned they will soon so outnumber us that all the advantages we have will not be able to preserve our language, and even our government will become precarious."[56]

It sounds like this may have been written in the late 1900s. But founding father Benjamin Franklin wrote this in 1753 because he feared the new German immigrants, who spoke a different language and had different customs from those he was used to. The US population totaled a little over a million people at that time, and the continent was mostly undeveloped, so there was plenty of room for new immigrants. But Franklin worried that the Germans would soon outnumber and impose their culture on the citizens who previously arrived from Great Britain. Had he relied on facts, such as the fact that new immigrants were helping to develop the new country, he would have realized there was plenty of room and a true need for these immigrants.

Similar fears led many native-born Americans to call for reducing or stopping immigration throughout the 19th and 20th centuries. "If America is to survive as 'one nation, one people' we need to call a 'time-out' on immigration,"[57] stated Patrick Buchanan in 1994. Buchanan's fears about immigrants overrunning native-born Americans also belie the fact that America's immigrant population actually shrank between the early and later parts of the 20th century. In 1990, only 7.9 percent of the population was foreign-born, compared to 14.8 percent in 1930. Again, facts prove that fears about being overrun with immigrants are unfounded.

Immigrants Are Needed to Fill Jobs

It is also a fact that the United States needs immigrants because of declining birth rates and rising life expectancy, meaning that fewer babies are being born and people are living longer. The birth rate for native-born Americans in the 1990s is about two births per woman, down from about three during the so-called baby boom years between 1946 and 1964, according to the Population Reference Bureau. At the same time, life expectancy increased from 66.6 years for men and 73.1 years for women in 1960 to 73.8 for men and 79.5 for women in 1998. This could leave the United States with a large aging population and not enough young people to sustain a healthy, productive economy.

A similar thing is happening in Japan because of low birth rates and very tight immigration restrictions. Japan's population started shrinking in the 1970s, and more and more jobs remain unfilled in the 1980s and 1990s. This is increasing wages and prices for goods and services and decreasing investment in Japanese businesses. At the same time, the number of elderly people keeps increasing, and workers must pay more in taxes to cover

Life expectancy is increasing in the United States while birth rates are dropping. With a growing aged population, young immigrants will be needed to sustain a healthy and productive economy.

increasing costs of health care for the aging population. Severe shortages of nurses and other health care professionals needed to care for elderly people have led the government to consider allowing in more foreign workers.

The birth rate in Japan is even lower than that among native-born Americans, as fewer Japanese people are marrying and having children. But even though the US population continues to increase because immigrants have higher birth rates, economists say more young immigrants are needed to take over jobs and create new businesses as more and more older workers retire. Studies show that immigrants also keep the economy healthy by spending money, paying taxes, and revitalizing dying inner-city areas. Immigrants, states an article by the Hoover Institution (a public policy think tank), "may contribute to the expansion of the labor market in cities by the purchases of goods and services, by forming their own businesses, and by saving dying industries, such as the textile industry in New York."[58]

> "If the United States is to maintain its position of leadership in the world, it will need a growing supply of highly skilled foreign-born workers."[59]
>
> —Economist Thomas Muller

And, in filling and expanding the job market, immigrants help America retain its position as a world leader, as economist Thomas Muller states in his 1993 book *Immigrants and the American City*: "If the United States is to maintain its position of leadership in the world, it will need a growing supply of highly skilled foreign-born workers."[59]

America Still Needs Immigrants

The need for immigrants to sustain a vibrant, prosperous America is especially important as the 20th century draws to a close. Many parts of the country have old, crumbling buildings, roads, and bridges that need repair or rebuilding. Since many Americans left these cities because of high crime rates and unemployment, new immigrants who need places to live and work have started rebuilding and breathing new life into these crumbling communities.

One place this is happening is in St. Louis, Missouri, where residents once described inner-city areas as ghost towns because of the many vacant and boarded-up homes and businesses. In the late 1990s about nine thousand refugee immigrants fleeing war-torn Bosnia settled in St. Louis and began transforming these neighborhoods into nice places to live. At first many older residents who stayed in these areas were wary of having so many new immigrants, according to Anna Crosslin, who heads a St. Louis refugee resettlement agency. But once the Bosnians revitalized homes and started new businesses, longtime residents stated that their arrival was "one of the best things that has ever happened to the city."[60] Similar things have happened in small rural towns like Greenport, New York; Denison, Iowa; and Huron, South Dakota, which have all been resuscitated by new immigrants from Central America and Asia. As economist Julian L. Simon notes, "The most important fact about immigrants is that they typically arrive when they are young and healthy"[61] and have the energy and drive to do things like rebuilding and revitalizing.

The experience in St. Louis and other cities is reminiscent of the poem called "The New Colossus," written by Emma Lazarus in 1883 and inscribed on a plaque inside the Statue of Liberty in 1903:

Give me your tired, your poor,

Your huddled masses yearning to breathe free,

The wretched refuse of your teeming shore.

Send these, the homeless, tempest-tossed to me,

I lift my lamp beside the golden door![62]

As the statue was the first thing many immigrants saw when their ships approached New York Harbor, it and the poem symbolized a sign of welcome to outsiders.

Nearly a hundred years later, America's role as a refuge is more important than ever as millions of people escape from oppressive governments, wars, and other catastrophes. President Ronald Reagan aptly described America's calling in his 1982 Christmas Day speech to the American people, in which he spoke about a letter he received from a US sailor stationed on the aircraft carrier *Midway* in the South China Sea. The letter described how navy personnel rescued sixty-five Vietnamese refugees floundering in a leaky boat. According to Reagan, these sailors represent what is great about America. "I know we're crowded and we have unemployment and we have a real burden with refugees, but I honestly hope and pray we can always find room,"[63] he said.

> "I know we're crowded and we have unemployment and we have a real burden with refugees, but I honestly hope and pray we can always find room."[63]
>
> —President Ronald Reagan in 1982

The role immigrants in the late 20th century are playing in revitalizing and keeping America's economy humming is reason enough to conclude there is room for more immigrants. But America's proud tradition as a nation of immigrants and a refuge for those seeking a better life is certainly also a sound reason to keep the door open. As historian Maldwyn Allen Jones puts it, immigration was America's "raison d'être,"[64] its reason for being.

America Had No Room
for New Immigrants

"The large number of immigrants now living here represents an enormous challenge. No nation has ever attempted to incorporate over 26 million newcomers into its society. Moreover, without a change in immigration policy, immigration's impact will only grow."

—Steven A. Camarota, Center for Immigration Studies research director

Steven A. Camarota, "Immigrants in the United States—1998," Center for Immigration Studies, January 1, 1999. https://cis.org.

Consider these questions as you read:

1. Do you agree with the idea that a country can reach the point of having too many people? Why or why not?
2. What is your view of an immigration policy that allows immigrants to sponsor other family members who wish to live in the United States? Explain your reasoning.
3. If you were a lawmaker, what type of immigration policies would you implement to balance the needs and wishes of American citizens with those of potential immigrants?

Editor's note: The discussion that follows presents common arguments made in support of this perspective. All arguments are supported by facts, quotes, and examples taken from various sources of the period or present day.

Twentieth-century America is overcrowded, and immigrants are making it even more so. Immigrants are also exacerbating the devastating environmental damage that results from human over-population. In addition the vast majority of Americans want immigration stopped or slowed significantly. For these reasons it is imperative for the US government to create policies aligned with the reality that there is no room for more immigrants.

America Is Overcrowded

America is overcrowded in the 20th century. Students are crammed into overcrowded classrooms. Cities and roads, bridges, and railroads strained by overpopulation badly need repairs and rebuilding. Millions of Americans are unemployed because there are too many people competing for too few jobs. Wildlife and the environment have been devastated by human overpopulation. And researchers find that immigration is largely responsible for this overpopulation. According to the Population Reference Bureau, immigrants and their offspring have caused the US population to triple during the 20th century (from 76 million in 1900 to 281 million in 2000). Between 1965 and 2000, immigrants have added at least a million and a half people per year, accounting for nearly 80 percent of the population growth. Allowing in more of the millions of immigrants who want to live in the United States would worsen all these consequences of overpopulation; thus, immigration must be curtailed.

In the early 1900s there were plenty of jobs and plenty of undeveloped open spaces, so there was a place for immigrants during those years. But by the time the huge influx of immigrants began in 1965, America was already overcrowded. What was once desirable became burdensome and undesirable, and American policy makers should have shut the door on immigration before these problems escalated. As former Colorado governor Richard Lamm stated in 1985, "Immigration has been good for America, but the public policy of immigration was made when we were an empty continent and could absorb unlimited amounts of unskilled labor."[65] Indeed, the disastrous effects of allowing mass immigration after 1965 led labor economist Vernon M. Briggs Jr. to write

> "Immigration has been good for America, but the public policy of immigration was made when we were an empty continent and could absorb unlimited amounts of unskilled labor."[65]
>
> —Former Colorado governor Richard Lamm

that the 1965 immigration laws were implemented without "any forethought . . . careful planning or public debate."[66]

Birth Rates

Social scientists find that two factors—high fertility rates among immigrants and millions of immigrants entering the country—have been driving the massive population increases in the United States during the 20th century. "The increase in U.S. births since 1970 has been driven entirely by births to immigrant mothers,"[67] according to a Pew Research Center study. In 1997 a typical native-born US family has two children, while immigrant families typically have three or more kids. These higher birth rates of millions of immigrant women make the American population growth rate skyrocket. Indeed, a study by the Center for Immigration Studies indicates that the number of births to immigrant mothers increased 272 percent between 1970 and 2002, adding nearly a million new babies to the population each year.

High birth rates and massive numbers of incoming immigrants do not just lead to unsustainable population growth in the United States. Studies show that high birth rates among immigrants also lead native-born Americans to decrease their own birth rates because they perceive their children will lose out to the many immigrants who are coming into the country. Sociologists noted this trend as early as 1901, when Edward Ross wrote that Americans "restrict the size of the family as the opportunities hitherto reserved for their children are eagerly snapped up by the numerous progeny of the foreigner."[68]

The second factor leading to an overcrowded country has to do with patterns of immigration. Often when one individual enters the United States, that person sponsors other family members who in turn bring yet more relatives. Some call this pattern chain migration. In one case a Filipino nurse received a temporary work permit in 1972 and soon achieved permanent resident status. This allowed her to bring in her parents as immigrants. After she became a citizen, she sponsored her nine brothers and sisters,

One factor causing overcrowded immigrant populations is known as chain migration. This is when one immigrant enters the United States, then sponsors a family member who in turn brings in more relatives.

and these brothers and sisters brought in their spouses, children, cousins, and so on. Eventually this nurse brought in forty-five family members. Chain migration among millions like her quickly adds tens of millions to the US population.

In 1997 demographer Leon Bouvier noted that since immigration is responsible for American overcrowding, "lowering immigration levels as soon as possible is the quickest way to end, or at least reduce, population growth."[69]

Heightened Environmental Pressures

As the number of people and the overcrowding in America keep increasing throughout the 20th century, the associated environmental problems also grow. According to population biology experts Paul Ehrlich and Anne Ehrlich, America became overcrowded when its population exceeded 75 million in the early

20th century, and the environmental effects steadily worsened after this milestone.

A 1996 report by the President's Council on Sustainable Development notes that chain migration, refugee resettlement, and a high birth rate among immigrants directly causes environmental damage that includes depletion of natural resources, pollution, massive species extinctions, and increased greenhouse gas emissions. As the population grows throughout the 20th century, people destroy natural habitats and deplete natural resources to build houses, roads, and other components of human expansion. According to wildlife biologist Winthrop Staples III and philosophy professor Philip Cafaro, the consequences of not stopping population growth will be catastrophic. "Continued mass immigration into the United States threatens the very existence of many nonhuman beings and species. . . . In order to seriously address environmental problems at home and become good global environmental citizens, we must stop U.S. population growth,"[70] they state.

The immigrant-driven effects of American population growth have been especially damaging in connection with climate change. When immigrants come to the United States, they are eager to reap the financial rewards of living in the land of opportunity and acquire habits like driving multiple cars, overusing electricity and water, and doing other things that increase greenhouse gas emissions. "The average immigrant, in coming to the U.S., quadruples their greenhouse gas emissions compared to their impacts in their sending country,"[71] explains a report by the Federation for American Immigration Reform. Slowing the flow of immigrants would lessen crowding and reduce impacts on the environment.

Americans Favor Less or No Immigration

American citizens have pleaded with lawmakers to severely limit or end immigration so the environmental and social effects of overpopulation can be more easily managed. Surveys find that anywhere from 70 percent to 86 percent of Americans support stricter limits on immigration. A 1995 poll by the organization Negative Population Growth found that 70 percent of respondents thought the total number of immigrants allowed into the United States each year should be less than 300,000. Fifty-four percent preferred fewer than 100,000, and 20 percent wanted zero immigrants. In 1995, when the poll was conducted, more than a million (legal) immigrants came to the United States. According to Bouvier, this poll provides overwhelming evidence that "a majority of Americans do consider population growth to be a major problem, one that should be addressed now. . . . [Most say] enough is enough."[72] Yet lawmakers refuse to implement the will of the people by reducing or stopping immigration. Instead, every immigration law enacted after 1964 has increased the number of immigrants who arrive each year.

Social scientists and policy experts point out that the US Constitution does not include anything about the right to immigrate to the country, and Americans concerned about their quality of life have a right to restrict the number of people who immigrate. "U.S. law in effect treats immigration as a sort of imitation civil right, extended to an indefinite group of foreigners who have been selected arbitrarily and with no regard to American interests,"[73] writes Peter Brimelow.

> "The simple truth is that we've lost control of our own borders, and no nation can do that and survive."[74]
>
> —President Ronald Reagan in 1984

In 1984 President Ronald Reagan warned that out-of-control immigration threatens America's very survival. "The simple truth is that we've lost control of our own borders, and no nation can do that and survive,"[74] he stated. Americans, including lawmakers, must realize that America's past as a magnet for immigrants is over, and the country will not survive unless its immigration policies reflect what is best for American citizens—not for outsiders who seek to better themselves at Americans' expense.

Source Notes

Chapter One: A Brief History of 20th-Century Immigration

1. David Heer, *Immigration in America's Future*. Boulder, CO: Westview, 1996, p. 1.
2. Quoted in The Heritage Guide to the Constitution, "Naturalization." www.heritage.org.
3. Quoted in Martin B. Gold, *Forbidden Citizens: Chinese Exclusion and the U.S. Congress*. Alexandria, VA: Capitol.Net, 2012, p. 18.
4. US Department of State, Office of the Historian, "The Immigration Act of 1924 (The Johnson-Reed Act)." https://history.state.gov.
5. Heer, *Immigration in America's Future*, p. 61.
6. Quoted in Pew Research Center, Hispanic Trends, "Chapter 4: U.S. Public Has Mixed Views of Immigrants and Immigration," September 28, 2015. www.pewhispanic.org.
7. Faye Hipsman and Doris Meissner, "Immigration in the United States: New Economic, Social, Political Landscapes with Legislative Reform on the Horizon," Migration Policy Institute, April 16, 2013. www.migrationpolicy.org.
8. Peter Brimelow, *Alien Nation*. New York: Random House, 1995, p. xviii.
9. Maldwyn Allen Jones, *American Immigration*, 2nd ed. Chicago: University of Chicago Press, 1992, p. 4.

Chapter Two: Did 20th-Century Immigration Harm the US Economy?

10. National Research Council, *The Immigration Debate: Studies on the Economic, Demographic, and Fiscal Effects of Immigration*. Washington, DC: National Academies Press, 1998, p. 87.
11. Lorraine M. McDonnell and Paul T. Hill, *Newcomers in American Schools: Meeting the Educational Needs of Immigrant Youth*. Santa Monica, CA: Rand Corporation, 1993. www.rand.org.

12. Quoted in Nicolaus Mills, ed., *Arguing Immigration: The Debate over the Changing Face of America*. New York: Touchstone, 1994, p. 35.
13. Jones, *American Immigration*, pp. 293–94.
14. Ufuk Akcigit, John Grigsby, and Tom Nicholas, "Research: Immigrants Played an Outsize Role in America's Age of Innovation," *Harvard Business Review*, April 21, 2017. https://hbr.org.
15. Council of Economic Advisers, "Immigration's Economic Impact," June 20, 2007. https://georgewbush-whitehouse.archives.gov.
16. David Bier, "What Happened to U.S. Wages During Mass Immigration?," Competitive Enterprise Institute, May 20, 2013. https://cei.org.
17. Heer, *Immigration in America's Future*, p. 191.
18. Quoted in Amy L. Wax and Jason Richwine, "Low-Skill Immigration: A Case for Restriction," *American Affairs*, vol. 1, no. 4, Winter 2017. https://americanaffairsjournal.org.
19. Quoted in Mills, ed., *Arguing Immigration*, p. 35.

Chapter Three: Did 20th-Century Immigration Worsen Crime?

20. Reports of the Immigration Commission, *Abstracts of Reports of the Immigration Commission: With Conclusions and Recommendations and Views of the Minority (in Two Volumes) (Presented by Mr. Dillingham)*. Washington, DC: US Government Printing Office, 1911.
21. John M. Murrin et al., *Liberty, Equality, Power*, vol. 2, 6th ed. Boston: Cengage Learning, 2012, p. 551.
22. Quoted in Association for Diplomatic Studies & Training, "A Flood of Cuban Migrants—the Mariel Boatlift, April–October 1980." http://adst.org.
23. Quoted in Avital H. Bloch and Servando Ortoll, "The Anti-Chinese and Anti-Japanese Movements in Cananea, Sonora, and Salt Lake River, Arizona, During the 1920s and 1930s," *Americana*, vol. 6, no. 1, Spring 2010. http://americanaejournal.hu.
24. Quoted in Nazgol Ghandnoosh and Josh Rovner, "Immigration and Public Safety," Sentencing Project, March 2017. www.sentencingproject.org.

25. National Commission on Law Observance and Enforcement, *Crime and the Foreign Born: Report No. 10*. Washington, DC: US Government Printing Office, 1931, p. 400.
26. Tim Wadsworth, "Is Immigration Responsible for the Crime Drop? An Assessment of the Influence of Immigration on Changes in Violent Crime Between 1990 and 2000," *Social Science Quarterly*, vol. 91, no. 2, June 2010.
27. Quoted in Jessica T. Simes and Mary C. Waters, "The Politics of Immigration and Crime," in *The Oxford Handbook of Ethnicity, Crime, and Immigration*, edited by Sandra M. Bucerius and Michael Tonry. New York: Oxford University Press, 2014, p. 459.
28. Quoted in Simes and Waters, "The Politics of Immigration and Crime," pp. 459–60.
29. Reports of the Immigration Commission, *Abstracts of Reports of the Immigration Commission*.
30. Quoted in Simes and Waters, "The Politics of Immigration and Crime," p. 460.
31. Carnegie Endowment for International Peace and the Urban Institute, "Immigration and the Justice System," *Research Perspectives on Migration*, vol. 1, no. 5, July/August 1997. http://carnegieendowment.org.
32. Quoted in Thomas A. Guglielmo, *White on Arrival: Italians, Race, Color, and Power in Chicago, 1890–1945*. New York: Oxford University Press, 2003, p. 77.
33. Quoted in US House of Representatives, "Depression, War, and Civil Rights: Hispanics in the Southwest," History, Art & Archives. http://history.house.gov.
34. Quoted in Neil Foley, *Mexicans in the Making of America*, Cambridge, MA: Belknap, 2014, p. 136.

Chapter Four: Did 20th-Century Immigration Threaten American Culture?

35. Samuel P. Huntington, *Who Are We?* New York: Simon & Schuster, 2004, p. 40.
36. Quoted in Christopher Harris, "Teddy Roosevelt's 'Unhyphenated America' Speech," Unhyphenated America, May 5, 2014. www.unhyphenatedamerica.org.
37. Arthur M. Schlesinger Jr., *The Disuniting of America: Reflections on a Multicultural Society*. New York: Norton, 1998, pp. 20, 22.

38. Huntington, *Who Are We?*, p. 164.

39. Huntington, *Who Are We?*, p. 159.

40. Patrick J. Buchanan, "Is America Still a Country?," August 8, 1997. http://buchanan.org.

41. Quoted in Vernon M. Briggs Jr., *Mass Immigration and the National Interest*. New York: Sharpe, 2003, pp. 3–4.

42. Stephen Webster, "Fade to Brown," American Renaissance, April 2003. www.amren.com.

43. James Davison Hunter, *Before the Shooting Begins: Searching for Democracy in America's Culture War*. New York: Free Press, 1994, p. 191.

44. Spencer P. Morrison, "Illegal Immigration Destroys American Schools, Hurts Kids the Most," *Investment Watch Blog*, January 24, 2018. http://investmentwatchblog.com.

45. Quoted in James Fallows, "Immigration: How It's Affecting Us," *Atlantic*, November 1983, www.theatlantic.com.

46. Patrick J. Buchanan, *State of Emergency: The Third World Invasion and Conquest of America*. New York: St. Martin's Griffin, 2006, p. 12.

47. Buchanan, *State of Emergency*, p. 11

48. Quoted in Great Seal, "E Pluribus Unum." http://greatseal.com.

49. Quoted Arthur M. Schlesinger Jr., "E Pluribus Unum?," in *American Culture: An Anthology*, 2nd ed., edited by Anders Breidlid et al. New York: Routledge, 2008, p. 62.

50. Quoted in Eric Freedman and Edward Hoffman, eds., *John F. Kennedy in His Own Words*. New York: Citadel, 2005, p. 24.

51. Quoted in Carl Degler, *Out of Our Past: The Forces That Shaped Modern America*. New York: Harper and Row, 1984, p. 322.

52. Charles Hirschman, "The Contributions of Immigrants to American Culture," *Daedalus*, vol. 142, no. 3, Summer 2013.

53. Pew Research Center, "Second-Generation Americans," February 7, 2013. www.pewsocialtrends.org.

54. Hirschman, "The Contributions of Immigrants to American Culture."

55. Hirschman, "The Contributions of Immigrants to American Culture."

Chapter Five: Did 20th-Century America Have Room for New Immigrants?

56. Benjamin Franklin, "Letter to Peter Collinson," TeachingAmericanHistory.org. May 9, 1753. www.teachingamericanhistory.org.

57. Patrick J. Buchanan, "Immigration Time-Out," October 31, 1994. www.buchanan.org.
58. Hoover Institution, "Immigration and the Rise and Decline of American Cities," August 1, 1997. www.hoover.org.
59. Thomas Muller, *Immigrants and the American City*. New York: New York University Press, 1993, p. 276.
60. Quoted in Matthew La Corte, "Refugees Are Revitalizing Some Great American Cities Facing Decline," *Huffington Post*, June 24, 2016. www.huffingtonpost.com.
61. Quoted in Mary H. Cooper, "Immigration Reform," *CQ Researcher*, vol. 3, no. 36, September 24, 1993.
62. Quoted in US National Park Service, "The New Colossus," Statue of Liberty, National Monument, New York. www.nps.gov.
63. Quoted in the American Presidency Project, "Ronald Reagan: Christmas Day Radio Address to the Nation," December 25, 1982. www.presidency.ucsb.edu.
64. Jones, *American Immigration*, p. 1.
65. Quoted in Mills, ed., *Arguing Immigration*, p. 17.
66. Vernon M. Briggs Jr., "Immigration and the U.S. Labor Market: Public Policy Gone Awry," Cornell University, ILR School, CAHRS Working Paper #92-41, 1992. http://digitalcommons.ilr.cornell.edu.
67. Gretchen Livingston, "5 Facts About Immigrant Mothers and U.S. Fertility Trends," Pew Research Center, October 26, 2016. www.pewresearch.org.
68. Edward Ross, "The Causes of Race Superiority," *Annals of the American Academy of Political and Social Science*, vol. 18, no. 1, July 1, 1901.
69. Leon Bouvier, "Americans Have Spoken: No Further Population Growth," Negative Population Growth, September 1, 1997. www.npg.org.
70. Winthrop Staples III and Philip Cafaro, "The Environmental Argument for Reducing Immigration to the United States," Center for Immigration Studies, June 17, 2009. https://cis.org.
71. Federation for American Immigration Reform, "U.S. Immigration and the Environment," September 2016. https://fairus.org.
72. Bouvier, "Americans Have Spoken."
73. Brimelow, *Alien Nation*, p. 5.
74. Quoted in the American Presidency Project, "Ronald Reagan: The President's News Conference," June 14, 1984. www.presidency.ucsb.edu.

For Further Research

Books

David M. Haugen, ed., *Illegal Immigration*. Farmington Hills, MI: Greenhaven, 2011.

Nick Hunter, *Immigration*. Portsmouth, NH: Heinemann, 2011.

Robert Morrow, *Immigration: Rich Diversity or Social Burden?* Minneapolis: Twenty-First Century, 2010.

Linda Barrett Osborne, *This Land Is Our Land: A History of American Immigration*. New York: Abrams Books for Young Readers, 2016.

Elizabeth Schmermund, ed., *Immigration Bans*. New York: Greenhaven, 2017.

Cath Senker, *Immigration*. London: Hachette Children's Group, 2011.

Tom Streissguth, *Welcome to America? A Pro/Con Debate over Immigration*. New York: Enslow, 2008.

Websites

American Immigration Council (www.americanimmigrationcouncil.org). The American Immigration Council is a nonprofit, nonpartisan organization that provides legal services to immigrants and advocates on their behalf in the area of public policy. Its website includes articles that explain the immigration system and laws, economic and other impacts of immigration, reforms, and more.

Aspiration, Acculturation, and Impact: Immigration to the United States, 1789–1930 (http://ocp.hul.harvard.edu/immigration.1.html). This web-based collection of historical materials from Harvard University's libraries, archives, and museums documents voluntary immigration to the United States through the start of the Great Depression. The collection includes a timeline, diaries, biographies, and other writings.

Center for Immigration Studies (https://cis.org). The Center for Immigration Studies is an independent, nonprofit research organization that publishes a variety of reports and articles that examine the social, economic, environmental, security, and economic consequences of both legal and illegal immigration. The CIS believes that debates informed by objective data will lead to better immigration policies.

Federation for American Immigration Reform (FAIR) (https://fairus.org). FAIR is a national, nonprofit organization of citizens who share the belief that America's immigration policies must be reformed to serve the national interest. FAIR seeks to stop all illegal immigration, favors greatly enhanced border security, and supports policies that would lower legal immigration levels.

Immigration: Primary Source Collections Online (https://shsulibraryguides.org/c.php?g=86715&p=558222). The Newton Gresham Library of Sam Houston State University in Texas offers a large collection of primary sources on many topics related to US immigration in the 20th century. The Bracero History Archive, Ellis Island records and photos, Minnesota immigrant oral histories, and more can be found on this site.

National Immigration Forum (www.immigrationforum.org). The National Immigration Forum advocates for immigrants and helps them navigate through the immigration system. It also educates the public about the value of immigrants and the ways in which sound immigration reform can benefit the United States.

Urban Institute (www.urban.org). The Urban Institute is a nonprofit research organization that seeks to educate the public on social issues like immigration and offer solutions to these issues. The organization conducts research on how immigration policies affect immigrants and the contributions of immigrants to America.

Index

Note: Boldface page numbers indicate illustrations.